Being: the bottom line

being:

the bottom line

nathan gill

NON-DUALITY PRESS

Deepest gratitude to Rose Youd for her hard work and
dedication in preparing this book

Non-Duality Press
6 Folkestone Rd, Salisbury SP2 8JP
United Kingdom
www.non-dualitybooks.com

First printing March 2006
Set in Plantin 11.5/14 & Rotis Serif
Cover design by John Gustard

www.nathangill.com

.

ISBN 978-0-9551762-2-7

In the year following publication of *Already Awake*, the focus of the talks began to shift to the theme of 'Being'. The present book is a selection from transcripts of live dialogues that emerged in the autumn of 2005.

Introduction

The bottom line is Being. Being awake or being asleep are actually beside the point.

Usually the idea is that dialogues such as these have the specific purpose of bringing about enlightenment, awakening, liberation—whatever the term used for that which is deemed to be escape from (or transcendence of) identification as a suffering individual. But our true nature is always Being and doesn't require any enlightenment or awakening. It simply *is* already, whether there's identification or not.

In the play of life, whenever there is identification, the story tends to be about improving *what is* in some way. And when that takes the form of the search for awakening, the focus usually falls on getting rid of the sense of individuality, as though it were somehow wrong or unreal.

But if there's a sense of individuality and a story about seeking to be rid of it, then precisely *that* is reality. Being has no requirements whatsoever. Nothing needs to be changed or attained in order to *be*. This present appearance is already the perfect expression of Being and cannot be avoided.

Table of Contents

A Description

Oneness, or Being, although indivisible, could be said to have two aspects: awareness, and the presently appearing content of awareness.

The content of awareness is all of the various images that appear: visual images, sensations, sounds, thoughts, feelings, etc. All these images appear presently in awareness, but the thought images appear to offer an added dimension, the capacity for seeming distraction away from or out of presence into the story of 'me' as an individual, a distinct entity located in time and space.

This story of 'me' is based in thought, and as thought is only part of the whole picture, when the story appears as reality there's an accompanying sense of lack. Seeking for wholeness is the story of the attempt to fill this sense of lack.

The search for wholeness arises in myriad ways, one of which is the search for enlightenment. Here too it is inevitably focused within the personal story, the partial, psychological view of reality, and consequently it cannot result in a lasting sense of fulfilment.

Whenever the play of life is not seen from the psychological viewpoint—from the point of view of 'my' story—there is a non-personalised, unfragmented picture free of any sense of lack.

Everything is likely to appear just as it did before, but without the distorted view that makes it 'mine'.

So what can be done to disengage attention from the personal story?

Nothing can be done, because there isn't actually any entity present that could do anything. The personal story is what gives the impression of a someone that's doing things, making choices, taking decisions, etc, whereas in actuality this someone, or 'me', is simply a commentary arising along with whatever else is appearing.

In the absence of the commentary, or where the commentary is seen as such, it's quite obvious that everything is happening or appearing entirely of its own accord. No one is doing anything.

But who sees it as a commentary?

All of the images are appearing, or being registered, in awareness. There's no one, no entity, to see it. All of this is simply happening in Being. The commentary has the effect of personalising the awareness aspect of Being, giving the *impression* of a someone where in fact there's no one.

This can be very frustrating, to hear that there's nothing to be done when there's still a sense of a someone that can do something.

Yes, whenever there's identification as a someone, there will be a corresponding feeling of agitation or frustration, the need to fill the sense of lack. Maybe seeking to fill that sense of lack takes the form of performing various practices such as enquiry or meditation, or maybe simply hearing a description about all of this is enough for seeking to be seen in its true light.

At those times when there's an understanding of that, there comes a real feeling of relief.

Understanding can certainly give rise to a profound sense of relief. But understanding (in the sense that I use the word) is still something integral to the story of 'me'.

But can't understanding also lead outside of the story, to enlightenment?

If the story is seen as a story then no understanding or anything else is needed to 'lead outside' of it.

So seeing through the story, or the disappearance of the story—is that enlightenment then?

'Enlightenment' only appears significant from the view-point of 'me'. Only the story of 'me' requires enlighten-ment. Your true nature is Being, and Being is already all that is (even when there is seeming ignorance of that) with no requirements whatsoever.

So even apparent ignorance of Your true nature is still the expression of Your true nature?

All ignorance and all stories about overcoming ignorance are the perfect expression of Being. It's impossible to avoid Being. How hard is it to *be*? It's always the case, regardless of what appears.

Various teachers prescribe methods and techniques that seem to produce results.

Yes, and just as often they *don't* produce results. It's an interesting story, isn't it?

So it all just happens as it happens? The teacher prescribing a technique, and the student practising the technique, and some result happening or not—that couldn't be otherwise?

Exactly so. Everything is happening entirely of its own accord because there actually isn't anyone to make anything happen. 'I' is part of what's happening, not the cause of any of it.

Everything may be happening of its own accord, and yet it often seems as though there's a 'me' making plans, taking decisions, doing things.

It's the commentary in thought that seemingly divides what appears into something being done by someone.
  But there's nothing wrong with that; it's not something that's got to go so that something else called enlightenment can take over. If there's identification, then that's what's happening, that's what appears as reality. If that identification is seen through, then *that's* what's happening. Being is already the case, whatever the configuration of appearances.

A sudden total dropping of identification of any kind could also happen of course.

Yes, that could happen mid-story.

But the identification could return?

Maybe, but any coming and going is merely the play of life. As far as Your nature as Being is concerned, the absence or presence of a personal self is inconsequential. Being simply *is*, and all of these appearances and happenings may simply be described as the cosmic entertainment. In actuality, nothing has ever happened.

Try to not *be*!

I wonder what you see as the purpose of this talk?

I don't see any purpose. A room is appearing with people in it. A conversation is happening, which appears to be in the form of a description. Maybe in the case of some of the characters some kind of relaxing happens in hearing this description, maybe not. It doesn't actually matter because the whole thing is simply happening in Being, *is* Being. Purpose or meaning appears within the story of individuality, and if that's what's happening, then that's fine as well.

So if you stop identifying, do you lose purpose?

It's not that 'you' stop identifying, but it's possible that the sense of identification that *is* 'you' disappears, and it may then be seen that no purpose is required to *be*. While the story of individuality is happening, purpose will usually seem significant; there's a sense of a 'me' going somewhere. That's the play of life.

The idea that there's no time never makes any sense to me.

Time is mesmerisation with the story in thought such that it appears significant, whereupon thoughts of past or future—which are actually only presently appearing ideas—are taken to be real. The only reality 'past' and 'future' have is in fact as ideas.

But the past did happen.

Nothing happened, though a thought may arise that says things happened.

I've still got the taste of biscuit and coffee in my mouth from half an hour ago.

That taste in the mouth is appearing presently, and along with the taste in the mouth arises a commentary that says, 'This taste is from half an hour ago'. There is no half-hour ago—there's only presence, and in presence there's a thought that includes the idea of half an hour ago. It's only thought that substantiates the idea of an individual 'me' extending through time.

So you're saying the taste is arising in presence with a story that's arising in presence, from nowhere—no causality?

Whenever there's identification with the story in thought, there appears to be time and cause and effect. Without identification, all is seen to be arising spontaneously, causelessly.

But it's not that either of these positions is 'right'. It's all Being, and no particular view is 'right' or 'wrong'. Where the search for enlightenment is promoted, however, it's suggested that the identified view is illusory. The description being given here is not biased in favour of an 'enlightened' view. I'm not trying to persuade you that you didn't eat a biscuit half an hour ago, but it's possible that that could be seen as a story rather than as a fact. Either way is reality.

Nothing needs to be 'got' or understood here. Life is just a play of images arising presently.

I can see that, but it's just that this 'I' seems so real. I can't seem to let go of it.

If it's what's appearing, then it *is* reality, it is real. No need to let go of it.

I've got no choice anyway.

No. Maybe identification will drop, maybe not. It's all Being. Being has no preference. If there was a preference, though, we'd have to say it's for confusion—because there's a lot more of that about than there is clarity!

(*laughter*)

Is Being an entity?

When it seems as though 'I' am an entity, then Being may also be presumed to be an entity of some kind, as some *thing* that can be acquired or attained. When there isn't identification as 'I', then there are no entities to be found anywhere.

So Being doesn't need an entity to experience itself?

Being is already the case, whatever is appearing.

So you can't not be?

Try to not *be*!

Sometimes I do! (laughter)

Simply this

So Nathan, very briefly—what's understanding, what's knowing, what's the difference between the two?

Understanding—in the way I use the term—is limited to thought; it appears as though there's someone trying to work it all out.

With knowing, thoughts still arise but they appear objectively in the same sense that a tree, a sound or a sensation appears. The story that their content conveys is not taken to be 'my' life, what 'I' am. Everything is simply as it is, with nothing needing to be worked out.

What's the difference between them? Understanding seems personal; knowing is impersonal. The difference is relative, though. Either way there's actually no one, there's simply *this*.

Thought

The nature of thought is such that it suggests other dimensions, other possible realities apart from *this*. If identification is the present reality and there is also present the *idea* of something called enlightenment, enlightenment in that example is illusory. It has no reality other than *as* an idea, as a thought. In that sense thought appears as the gateway out of presence, out of reality.

Isn't thought itself reality, though?

Thought may be appearing presently as part of reality, but when thought takes centre-stage in the play of life, its content suggests that there are endless alternatives to what presently *is*. It lends a seeming reality to the idea of past and future—what has happened, what might happen.

When thought is not viewed in that way, then there is simply this: everything as it presently appears. Which also includes thought.

Assumptions

The general theory is that rays of light come in through our eyes and form images in our heads, in our brains. But you're saying this is an unnecessarily complicated way of describing things. Is that correct?

Based on present evidence alone, on actuality, where is the brain that's supposedly inside this head? Are there any brains presently appearing in awareness?

There may be a book on the shelf that tells a story about there being brains inside these heads, where chemical reactions are happening and thoughts are being produced, but actually, right now, how many brains are there appearing in the room? *(laughter)* So presently, the brain story is based entirely on assumption.

But isn't this a limited view? It seems to me that you're say-ing that the brain and the story are less real than that which is presently perceived. Maybe a world without conceptual thought would be the reality for a tiny baby, but that's not reality for me. My reality includes all my stories, my experi-ences, my thoughts and all the rest of it. But I hear you say that all those thoughts, stories, etc, are less important and less real than the actual.

Whatever appears presently as reality *is* reality. I'm not suggesting any version of reality is more or less important than any other. What I am suggesting is that whatever presently appears as reality can be seen in an entirely different way when not based on a thought-filtered view.

But there is a brain. It's the brain that keeps on thinking these thoughts and analysing all the time, moving us from place to place, running our lives and producing all these stories.

But does it? Is there really a brain that's thinking thoughts? Based on present evidence alone, thoughts are just appearing here in awareness. That there is a brain thinking thoughts is itself just another thought that arises as a story in awareness.

If you'd never heard all of these stories about brains being responsible for thoughts, then thoughts would simply be appearing mysteriously in awareness, with no brains to be seen anywhere. In fact, that's actually the case right now; that's what I'm pointing out. Going on present evidence, the brain as an instrument for producing thoughts inside these heads is just an assumption.

It's not that this assumption is 'wrong'. But the brain example serves to reveal how easily overlooked is the obvious fact that thought—and everything else—is simply appearing presently in awareness. Instead, when life is viewed through a filter of thoughts, of unexamined assumptions, endless stories explaining how and why everything appears are taken as reality.

When all of these assumptions *aren't* being taken as reality, when these thoughts are seen as thoughts, then everything still appears in awareness. Thoughts still arise, but their content doesn't have the effect of fractionating and dividing. In this case the stream of thought is merely an interesting story.

Let's say we've got a switch here which can instantly turn off the sound volume of the thoughts so that there's no longer a commentary running, no longer any stories appearing. Without that commentary there's simply what presently appears in awareness—which still includes thoughts, although they're now inaudible. With the *content* of thought no longer available, whatever presently appears is viewed directly, rather than in the fractionated way in which the thought story presents it.

I'm not saying that thoughts have to disappear from the picture, but that if their content isn't viewed in a serious light, then life appears as more of an entertainment than an ordeal.

But if you drop all of the assumptions, everything disappears.

Does it? You're a step ahead of me then. *(laughter)* There are no assumptions arising here right now, and yet everything still appears.

But you're actually speaking from the position of a baby. This is how a baby sees things, without all these assumptions. But to have faith in not investing in the stories that appear requires us to let go of everything that we are, everything that we seem to be.

I'm not suggesting that you have faith in anything— merely that it's possible for this life to happen without assumptions. It's the assumptions that require faith!

So is this why it's said that when the thought story isn't taken as reality and there's no past, no history, everything seems new and fresh in each moment? That's what the difference between you and me is. I'm seeing it as samey and boring but you're seeing it as ever fresh.

For as many characters as there are in the room there are that many versions of reality, and no one version of it is more significant than any other. So if what presently appears is the same old table and a rather unremarkable standard lamp, then that's what is. That's reality.

But if you're enlightened you don't mind.

There you go with the assumptions again! *(laughter)*

The television screen of life

If the 'me' disappears, it does so entirely spontaneously.

The fact that you say that can seem to imply that the absence of the 'me' is preferable. Actually it doesn't matter, does it?

If the 'me' disappears, it's simply what's happening on the screen of life.

So just like when you change the channel on the television and you find there's a more enjoyable programme showing?

Exactly. Whether there's identification or whether there's liberation, both of them are appearing in the movie of Being.

Liberation

Is there liberation in the story?

Inherent in the story is the implication that there's someone who can be liberated, but actually there's no one.

What I mean, I guess, is within the story are there characters who appear to be liberated?

Anything can happen in a story. Consciousness, or Being, appears as this great play—or perhaps we could call it a movie—of life. Being is the movie and the screen, all of the characters, all of the stories. The movie is seen from the viewpoint of the characters, 'liberated' or not, and 'liberated' characters in the movie speak of freedom from identification with the story of 'me'.

Actually, there's no one and nothing anywhere that needs liberation. The movie runs its course but nothing ever really happens. In that sense, what significance does liberation have?

But in the movie it's made out to be significant.

Being is Your nature, and the movie in all of its glorious un-enlightenment is how You appear to Yourself. Why not include some thrilling storylines about liberation?

Or winning the lottery.

That would be too much to hope for! (laughter)

Avoiding feeling

Hearing and reading about non-duality has for me been a way of avoiding feeling; I've tried to use it as a way to escape from the ordinariness and messiness of being human. The desire has been to become pure awareness and to avoid fully embracing being everything, especially the painful emotional bits.

It seems to me that emotions reinforce the feeling of separation and encourage the search for oneness. I built up a perfect understanding to escape the uncertainty and suffering of emotional pain, and for a while that worked; I managed to avoid the emotional issues that troubled me. I guess I thought that my excellent understanding was making me immune from them. But it didn't last, and when I began to suffer again, I was confused.

I see now, though, that my story is a story of trying to escape from emotional suffering and being forced through the failure of that strategy to be with everything equally.

When feeling arises accompanied by a thought story, that's what is referred to as emotion. The colouring and fractionating of feeling by the story in turn gives the story added life; it makes it seem more vivid and real.

Your particular story is that the character is forced out of understanding by emotional crises. Understanding is based in thought, part of the story, but the story that is understanding is easily swept away by the more compelling combination of feeling and story that constitutes emotion.

In the arising of feeling without the accompanying 'hook' of a story, any sense of dilemma is absent, and it's quite clear that feeling is simply intrinsic to the rich tapestry of Being.

In hearing this described objectively, there's a relaxing out of trying to change anything—which makes life seem more effortless, even if there's still discomfort. Escaping from that discomfort is what previously motivated my pursuit of understanding.

I can see now, though, that whatever way these crises are dealt with in a particular character's story—maybe going to a therapist, pursuing understanding or doing self-enquiry—is exactly appropriate for the playing out of that story. But it's not going to lead to enlightenment, is it?

Maybe in one character's case, understanding or self-enquiry *does* appear to give rise to the untangling of story from feeling, but for another character there may be no inclination whatsoever to engage in anything of that nature.

This play of life isn't about arriving ultimately at the recognition of Your true nature via enquiry or whatever means, although it may include that as a possibility. Life is already perfect in all of its seeming imperfection, whether that's seen or not.

So even the focus in understanding isn't really the avoidance of what is?

No, there's *only what is. What is* can't possibly be avoided.

Thanks, Nathan. It's helpful for me to hear this hammered out time and time again, and given that in my case there's such a compulsion to chase understanding and use the intellect, particularly to hear that I don't have to do anything about it. Over the years I've tried everything—it's the struggling to do something about it all which seems to have been half the problem.

Practice

Doesn't our true nature need to be experientially realised through practice?

If the impulse to practise arises, then a life dedicated to practice may unfold. What would be realised, though?

Oneness, non-separation.

And who would realise that?

Well ... no one.

And the realisation would be that all along there's actually been no individual to become realised.

Yes.

So there isn't actually anyone here anyway who can have a need for realisation. Rather is it the case that the urge towards realisation through practice is merely one possible theme arising within the cosmic *lila*.

I can see that in theory, but unless oneness is realised through practice, surely the impulse will persist.

Maybe so. But it's also possible that the futility of practice might be revealed, either in the spontaneous falling away of the sense of individuality or through

31

understanding. As many characters indicate, the failure of practices to produce any kind of result is also a possibility.

But surely the realisation of our true nature is what everyone is evolving towards.

Evolution is a story. Being is already Your true nature—whether that's recognised or not. Being appears as every character, and in the vast majority of characters the main impulse is more towards survival—or saving up for a holiday!—than it is towards realisation.

There's always going to be a sense of lack until realisation happens, though.

There may be a sense of lack, but is that necessarily due to there being something missing? It could just as easily be said that performing practices in accordance with a story about future realisation is itself what presently gives rise to the very sense of lack it seeks to eradicate!

Present moment awareness

How can I stay in present moment awareness?

How can you leave it? There's only present awareness.
It's what You are, and what 'you' appear 'in'.

Tell me a story

Has the way you experience emotions changed?

There's simply *this*, where all appearances are *only* changing.

I mean in your life as a character.

You mean you want me to tell you a story! *(laughter)* Maybe about how Nathan was a character who was suffering and seeking, and then something called liberation happened, which gave rise to his experiencing emotions in a different way.

Yes, tell me a story then about how the experiencing of emotions has changed for Nathan.

No, because you're going to take it seriously. You're trying to get an answer under false pretences! *(laughter)*

If there's the sense of being a 'me', and something called anger arises in relation to some event or other, then the story that accompanies it appears to have validity—'You deliberately broke my favourite vase!' Resentment may then linger.

When reality isn't ascribed to the sense of individuality, the arising of anger or whatever isn't 'emotional'. It's not about how something is affecting 'me', and it passes as swiftly as it arose, without any residual story of grudge or resentment.

Seen in this way, it's simply another event arising in the play of life.

Avoiding the void

I've lived a life of constant striving, of running from something or towards something, always keeping on the move. It feels as though if I stop that constant activity I'll be swallowed up in a great dark void of misery, bitterness, fear, guilt, despair, rage. I can't afford not to have a purpose. It feels unsafe to relax. And yet in spite of this, in many ways I've also lived a very full life, a life that would be viewed by society in general as one that has combined great material achievement with help to others. I make friends easily. I've travelled the world. Many doors have opened for me. There have been some short periods of great joy, of a complete relaxing out of the misery of this constant chase. But always it returns.

I've spent time with famous teachers, attended extreme enlightenment intensives; there were some temporary highs, and I met many good and interesting people. But the permanent relief I was looking for has always eluded me.

About a year ago, I found myself at a Tony Parsons meeting. Soon afterwards, I heard about your own talks so I came along to see you as well. What you were both saying was a radical departure from everything else I'd been involved in, and I threw myself into attending all of yours and Tony's talks and retreats. I really resonated with what you both said in your respective approaches to addressing the immanence of Being, and initially was relieved and newly hopeful.

I could see the futility of striving, but at the same time, because of my fear of being swallowed up in the abyss of despair, I couldn't let go of it. To relax in presence just wasn't even a consideration, because relaxing only promised a fate worse than death. From my involvement over the years with psychology, philosophy and spirituality, I understood what the void in its various guises represents, but the terror inherent in my own version of the void wasn't something that I'd ever been able to dissipate through therapy, understanding, enquiry or surrender.

For the first time in my life I found myself adrift without a purpose, and this resulted in a terrible depression, the likes of which I had occasionally experienced before and always striven to avoid. I began to sink deeper into this and barely managed to conduct my daily affairs. Although they offered no comfort, I still came to yours and Tony's meetings. I had nowhere else to go.

I've kept my usual brave face on things, though, and now a new circle of friends has come into being, thanks to my attendance at the various talks and retreats, and I'm keeping occupied with business, social life and some body-based therapies. The void still threatens but it has receded into the background again. I feel compelled to continue seeking enlightenment—but I also understand the futility of that.

I've been everywhere and tried everything. I don't know what more I can do.

You've been everywhere and tried everything in your search for enlightenment without even questioning the idea that enlightenment is the answer. The search itself compounds the desperation. You're constantly running from something, towards something, without questioning whether the running itself has any validity.

But I have to keep moving, I have to have a purpose—otherwise I might fall into the void. It feels as though there's a question I could ask—if only I knew what it was and how to formulate it—and if I got the right answer, it would be so big, so massive that it would give me the insight I need for awakening to happen.

This perfect question and answer thing is all part of the running, and the running is about getting to a place where you can stop and simply *be*. But Being already *is*. You already *are*. This story of running is happening in Being.

The story feels relevant; it feels as though I am this story.

Yes, the 'I' is the story, it's inseparable from the story. And so long as there's mesmerisation, then the story appears as reality.

But what can I do to stop it?

'I' can't stop it. 'I' *is* the story. While there's mesmerisation, it seems as though 'I' am an entity living in a time-based reality, and that reality might include fear, despair, misery, as well as the attempt to escape from those things by awakening or becoming enlightened. But this awakening is just another projected event in the time-based story.

'I' can never escape from the story of 'I'—but it's possible that the story might be seen *as* a story, whether that appears to happen through various practices or entirely spontaneously. Regardless of appearances, though, no one *makes* it happen. No one is doing anything.

So some outside agency needs to operate.

There is no outside agency. There's simply Being.

This is so frustrating. If only there was something I could do. I find myself straining at the talks, listening intently, trying to find the perfect question, worrying that I might miss something important.

No further understanding is required. The story of your life is that there's always a straining for more of everything. Being is already the case under all circumstances. As far as your story is concerned, relaxing from the constant running that's been the story would reveal that it's not so much enlightenment that's needed as a good rest!

It feels as though I should be accomplishing something, something that would bring an about-face in the way I approach life.

There's been a whole life story of accomplishments, none of which has given any real peace, the sense that it's OK to simply *be*. Presently the scales are still tipping in favour of involvement with the story of seeking and running, but now there's nowhere left for that search to go. So maybe the scales will tip in the other direction. This isn't going to happen as a result of further effort and striving, though.

But I never actually did anything, did I?

Don't be concerned with getting the understanding right. If there seems to be a personal self here and there's involvement in a story of a lifetime of suffering, seeking and running, then maybe the futility of all that will come to be seen, such that more and more there's a life of relaxation. Maybe that personal self disappears—maybe not. But in a life unfolding simply in presence, would it even matter anymore?

Well, I've got nowhere left to go. Maybe what you say will become obvious, but I guess in the meantime I'll just have to keep limping on.

Escaping

There does seem to be something like a progression, the fact that I'm sitting here now listening to this message, which is so radical compared to the things that we were all fumbling about with twenty years ago. To say, 'Well, that's just meaningless' seems somehow wrong.

Look at the reality of the situation here: a room is appearing, with people in it. 'Twenty years ago' is a story. And the idea that something will be different in another ten years' time—that's also a story. The only reality there is is what presently appears.

We can get into a story of how things have progressed in twenty years and how they might progress in future. But actually, that would only be words coming out of a mouth presently, ideas arising in thought presently.

And that's commonly how this life is lived: in thought, in distraction from presence, from the simple presence of *this*, everything that's appearing here presently.

It would be unbearable, though, wouldn't it, not to escape every now and then into thought, to be constantly in presence, to be forced to stay awake?

What presently appears as unbearable is the idea that this everyday life of 'me' is all there is. Further ideas then arise about the necessity of escaping from this in some way. When there isn't distraction in thought, though, when thought is seen for what it is, then there is simply *this*: thoughts appearing here, images arising, sensations arising.

Would you be able to hold a conversation with such a person, though? (laughter) I mean, if they weren't allowed to go into thoughts.

Conversations happen whether there's distraction in thought or not. If thoughts are seen as thoughts, there can still be engagement with stories about past and future, but they don't offer any possibility of apparent escape from presence. It's obvious that there's nowhere to go.

'You' are only a thought

What is the certainty you have that means that you can be sitting at the front answering questions, while I'm back here wondering about it all?

Presently thoughts are taking centre-stage in the play of life and suggesting that there's a Nathan there who is certain and a 'me' here who lacks certainty. When thought takes centre-stage, when the story of 'me' is hogging the show, the sense of individuality—and the idea that there are other individuals—takes on an apparent solidity.

But there's no one *inside* these images: they *are* simply images, arising and passing in awareness.

In fact, Nathan doesn't have any certainty because there's no one 'in here' who could be certain—just as there's no one in 'you' to be uncertain.

'You' are only a thought.

Understanding

If a person has excellent understanding, does it really matter that there is still a subtle sense of identity there?

Whatever is happening is limited to the play of life, the play of appearances, so nothing *actually* matters. But if—within the play—there's excellent understanding which doesn't waiver even in relation to any crisis that arises in the life of the character, then no, it doesn't matter. It's merely that with understanding there's the potential for suffering because some sense of identity—however subtle that is—still remains.

Does that mean the life of that character would be lived in ease and comfort?

It could be—why not? To all intents and purposes the 'I' is absent.

So under such circumstances there wouldn't be any concern about finally getting rid of the 'I'?

Why should there be? Trying to finally get rid of the 'I' might appear to create problems where there weren't any.

So if the 'I' did actually disappear under those circumstances it maybe wouldn't even be noticed.

Maybe not. If the 'I' should disappear when to all intents and purposes it's already absent, then why should it be noticed? If there's already a life of ease, it wouldn't necessarily become *more* easeful.

So if my life is relatively OK, there needn't really be any concern about getting rid of the 'I'—because that concern itself seems to be the biggest problem I have!

Go away and live an ordinary life then. All of this is just nitpicking really, isn't it? If the 'I' disappears, then it does so entirely spontaneously anyway, not as a result of anything the 'I' does. If that's really understood then you can leave it all alone and do whatever else you like.

So what?

Twenty-five years ago I was travelling in Asia and I became mildly interested in Buddhism. So when I got back to the UK and heard that a Buddhist centre was starting up a few miles away from where I lived, I thought I'd give it a try. And for the next twenty years, Buddhism and the search for enlightenment took over my life.

The Buddhist teaching that all things are transient, unsatisfactory and devoid of a central essence or self seemed to make perfect logical sense, and the idea that an escape from the unsatisfactoriness of life was possible I found really exhilarating. In the early days of the centre the teacher would say things like 'Everything is perfect as it is', 'You are all enlightened already', 'There are no "shoulds", "oughts" or "musts" in reality'—not a million miles away from the kind of things you or Tony Parsons might say.

Over the years, however, the simplicity of the central message and the sense of inspiration seemed to become increasingly overshadowed by the emphasis on all the things that had to be done—or not done—if enlightenment was ever to occur. The sense of mystery and wonder got buried under a grim determination to confront and wrestle with the negativities that I came to believe were clouding my vision.

Having been well and truly hooked in by then, though, I could only keep going. My teacher would tell us that so long as we applied ourselves to the path with dedication, so long as we worked at developing the clarity of mind that would cut through confusion and reveal things as they truly are, it might take more than a single lifetime but we'd definitely get there in the end.

And for a long, long time I believed him. Why not? So far as I could tell, he was enlightened himself, so surely he must know more about what it took to 'get there' than I did. And if I didn't seem to be making much progress—or any progress at all—then clearly the fault must lie in my own application.

Eventually it began to dawn on me—and the realisation took a long time coming—that the problem didn't necessarily lie in my own inadequacy or lack of commitment. Perhaps, just perhaps, it was rather the case that the method itself was inherently flawed: it couldn't actually deliver what it promised.

At the end of 1999, I left the centre that had been my life for eleven years and struck out on my own. I found a job and a place to live and I gradually built myself a 'normal' life in the world. Thoughts about enlightenment, however, the idea that there must *be something other than the daily grind, the inexorable decline into sickness and death, continued to nag away at me.*

The following autumn I was in Watkins Bookshop in London. Attracted simply by the bizarreness of the author's name, I picked up a book by Wayne Liquorman. Even in my heavy Buddhist days, I'd always loved Nisargadatta's I Am That, *and I found Wayne's take on non-dualism attractive. A few months later I went to one of his weekends in London. Although I was wary of his emphasis on the guru-disciple relationship, I would probably have carried on seeing him if he hadn't lived over the other side of the world.*

Not long after, a friend happened to lend me a copy of The Open Secret. *I can't pretend that I understood it all, but something about the simplicity of Tony Parsons' words intrigued me. I took a look at his website and found that he was giving a talk in Salisbury the following Saturday.*

Tony's clarity and constant pulling the rug from under my feet have been an inspiration. He reawakened me to the mystery and the wonder of it all. He helped me to appreciate more and more that there is no one—therefore no choice and no responsibility. After all those years of continually trying to do the right thing and stop myself from doing the wrong thing, this came as such a relief.

How did what Tony said differ from what you'd heard before?

Tony was saying that everything is right as it is, and that there is in fact no one, no self. And that seemed to be exactly what my Buddhist teacher had been saying. For a while, I was quite confused about what the difference was, but gradually it became clearer that essentially it boiled down to a question of emphasis.

I've read somewhere that there are two basic approaches to enlightenment or liberation or whatever you want to call it: transcendence and immanence. Transcendence says we have to make the effort to go beyond the world to find the answer—immanence says the answer is already always present.

While the Buddhist teaching certainly includes the idea of immanence, what it really emphasises (in my experience of it, at least) is transcendence. So while anatta *or non-self is one of the central tenets of the teaching, and while it's said that enlightenment is totally beyond action and result, beyond time and space, beyond the conditioning process, you tend to hear more about the million and one things that can and must be done if you're ever to get to the point where enlightenment occurs and it can be seen that there is no self.*

Buddhism does recognise this contradiction, and it seems to address it by saying that you need to use the self to go beyond the self and by explaining that there are different levels of reality which should not be mixed. (There's 'conventional' reality where I am born, grow old and die and can choose the actions I take, 'ultimate' reality where there are just transient sensory phenomena, and beyond both of these, enlightenment itself. Complication upon complication ...)

Of course, all the emphasis on effort and control inevitably brings in its wake all the problems of comparison and perceived inadequacy that arise when characters who emotionally believe they are real and solid strive to come to the realisation that they aren't. So however often I managed to be mindful of self-doubt or conceit or even the concept of self arising, that did nothing to dent the emotional conviction that there actually was *a 'me' who could make progress on the path.*

Tony cut away all that. He dissolved that division between 'right' and 'wrong' and revealed that everything *is actually OK.*

The initial burst of euphoria lasted till I managed to dig myself into a pit of what amounted to fatalism. I'd heard Tony say time and time again when someone complained that his message seemed fatalistic, 'It's not that there is nothing that can be done—rather is it that there is no one'. On an intellectual level—and at times on an experiential level too—that made perfect sense. But increasingly I was getting bogged down in an emotional belief that there was nothing 'I' could do. Which of course led at times to intense feelings of futility and frustration, because I no longer had a direction in which to focus in order to resolve this dichotomy—Tony had taken it away from me!

When I was involved in Buddhism, at least there had always been something I could do—*be more mindful, meditate more, practise restraint. Now, despite everything Tony said about there being no one, despite my own intellectual understanding of that, my emotional reality was of a 'me' trapped in a situation that was hopeless.*

So you mean you started out, through Buddhism, with a positive, hopeful 'I can do something' approach, but then you found you'd gone to the opposite pole and were caught in the negative frustration of 'I can do nothing'?

Yes, exactly. And to make matters worse, where Buddhism gives you the impression that only one in a million ever gets enlightened, in the new non-dualist circles I was coming into contact with there seemed to be continual gossip and rumours about people waking up or 'getting it'. The satsang circuit was littered with new names, and it looked as though there would soon be more teachers than students. Which, in my worst moments, threw me right back into the sense of inadequacy of being someone who hadn't *'got it' and who doubtless never would get it.*

At first I tended to take the claims on trust but my sceptical streak gradually re-surfaced. A fellow sceptic summed it up when he reckoned that many of them were simply overreacting to what amounted to 'having a good day'!

So what's been happening more recently then?

Well, having been oscillating for some time between a frustrated, hopeless fatalism and an attitude of 'bugger the whole thing and turn on the tele', something you said at one of your talks recently really seemed to strike home. I know I've heard similar things from both you and Tony in the past, but this time the words got through.

It went something like this:

'At the talks we keep hearing "There's no one there" and this becomes another focus for seeking, as though it mattered in some way, that there ought to be no one here. Sometimes it can be completely obvious: we take a look and we see that there isn't actually anyone here. But if we take a look and there still seems to be someone, so what?'

That made me realise how much investment I'd been putting into the times when there seemed to be no one: 'being no one' is good and to be sought after, 'being me' is definitely not OK. And rather than the 'so what?' being a bolshie, frustrated kind of 'so what?' (along the lines of 'If I can't win this game, I'm not going to play it'), there was a feeling that whether there was no one, whether there was someone—it really didn't matter.

But then that vision or whatever you call it disappeared, and on the emotional level, being 'me' felt like a problem again.

But what you had said had revealed that I was still subtly hoping that a point would come when there would simply be 'Being' without any 'me-ing', that there would always be that experience of 'There is no one'. Much as I'd like that to be the case (!), you made it clearer to me that that just isn't necessary.

So I guess it's a bit like Pandora's box—hope's the last thing out!

Absolute stillness and relative striving

It's so beautiful, just to rest in Being. A few insights have happened recently—I don't want to attribute any significance to them, but now, when anything happens that previously would have hooked me into the story, it just doesn't stick any more.

That's nice. In Being there are endless possibilities, and every character in the room will present a unique version of reality. It's all happening in Being, though, so one version isn't more significant than any other.

But surely this is the goal of all seeking, to come to rest without the need for anything?

Where there's seeking, it's not leading to anything. Seeking is integral to the story of separation. The idea that it's leading somewhere is part of the story.

This is what's spoken of as liberation, though, the absence of the sense of individuality, everything appearing and disappearing with nothing to stick on to any more.

Whatever appears does so spontaneously and not as a goal that's achieved at the end of seeking. Being is equally present as the identified individual.

But for that identified individual there will still be a seeking to come to rest.

Yes, that story of identification contains the idea of coming finally to rest as a result of seeking. But whatever appears does so spontaneously. Whether there's seeking or not, Being has no end goal of coming to rest; that's just the story in the play. Being is all resting and all striving. Being is all that is. The actual appearance of the play is its only significance—not any happening within it.

I'm talking about the absolute stillness of Being, the absolute resting.

This conversation is a relative happening in the play. Awake or asleep, resting or striving, 'I' or no 'I'—none of this is significant; it's just the subject matter of the play. Yes, Being is absolute stillness—it's also, as I said, relative striving.

I can understand that you don't want to give any significance to anything that the seeker can fasten on to, but the absence of seeking is totally different to seeking!

This talk is a description with no agenda to promote non-seeking or to undermine seeking, although either could appear to happen.
   You seem to be agitated.

Well, you're on my case! I was only making an observation about what's happening here.

(Pause)

Ah! (laughs) I see what you're getting at. The 'me' position was readopted then, in taking a particular stance.

Yes. The 'me' isn't a fixed object—it's simply a thought, psychological identification. When thoughts are seen to be merely arising and passing away and there isn't identification with any particular thought or idea, then there's no relative position that constitutes 'me' as a separate entity. There's simply resting in Being, whether that's described as beautiful, delicious or boring.

And it's not that the 'me' is the enemy. It's just that, as you've said, where there is identification as 'me', then there's likely to be seeking in one form or another, a seeking to come to rest in the absence of identification.

Laughing at the news

I came to one of your talks a month or so ago, and the other day I found myself watching an apparently tragic item on the news and laughing uncontrollably.

Right, so is there maybe an assumption there that one of the outcomes of all of this is that world events aren't taken seriously anymore?

Well, yes. When you take yourself to be a separate person, then emotionally upsetting events are disturbing and unpleasant. But surely if you come to understand that everything is yourself, then there can't be any tragedy, because it's only your own self it's happening to.

So there's the understanding that everything is yourself?

Yes.

Isn't that just a story in thought, though? Because understanding is limited to thought, however sublime the nature of that understanding might be.

But you say that everything is happening of its own accord, so understanding isn't something that I'm doing—it's just happening! (laughter)

You can come and take the chair if you like! (*laughter*)

But spontaneously arising though it may be, understanding is just more 'stuff' that's added to the sum total of what constitutes the life of 'me'. There's nothing at all wrong with that, or with your uncontrollable laughter at a tragic event. As you point out: all of that is simply happening, no one is doing it, the tragedy isn't actually happening to anyone.

To provide a more comprehensive picture, though, I'd like to offer the possibility that—so far as the play of life is concerned—an apparent reaction of sadness or tears to tragic events is actually a very natural thing. There's nothing wrong with it at all. There's nothing wrong either with an *absence* of emotional reaction to a tragedy—or even an 'inappropriate' reaction such as laughter. But that's not somehow more 'spiritual' or 'enlightened'.

So as you've pointed out, sometimes there might be an 'inappropriate' response to events in life. But generally the nature of the play of life is such that tragic events will elicit sadness, even tears, whether there's no one or apparently someone, whether there's clarity, understanding or confusion.

I'm not suggesting, of course, that there actually are any entities who are perceiving or are caught up in tragedies, but whether there's a psychological sense of self playing centre stage or whether it's seen that there's no one here, in the spontaneous arising of appearances within this play of life certain patterns emerge.

It's possible either to understand or for there to be clear seeing that everything is happening spontaneously, no one is doing anything, no one is responsible, no one is being harmed. But if you find spontaneous laughter happening at a funeral, don't be surprised if you receive a spontaneous punch in the mouth! (laughter)

Cornwall correspondence

Dear Nathan

A few years ago I came across Clarity *and it immediately struck a chord, although I didn't fully understand it at the time. Having now read* Already Awake *and listened to your two CDs, it's as if a final stubborn obstacle seems to have been removed (although it is also seen that, in a sense, there never was an obstacle).*

I had for some time been equating awareness with what you could call present moment attention (being in the now, etc). I see now that this effort to 'be in the now' just creates more dualism, and that present moment awareness is simply a mind technique that subtly helps to reinforce the sense of a 'me'. Because whether the mind is attentive or not, presence is always the case.

While re-reading Already Awake *recently, I jotted down: 'Distraction and forgetfulness are the story of distraction and forgetfulness presently arising.' With this came a great sense of release.*

But a question has arisen:

We are already awake. Therefore it seems that what is traditionally referred to as awakening boils down to whether or not this 'already awakeness' is recognised. Is it not the case that this recognition (or remembrance) is simply a process of the mind, just as when we recollect where misplaced car keys are? The fog of non-recognition descended when we were tiny children and has been reinforced ever since through all kinds of conditioning, etc. Isn't this fog essentially all mind stuff?

Dear --------

It's not that 'we' are already awake—rather it's that
Your true nature is the *awakeness* in which all presently
appears.

Did any fog of non-recognition descend when you
were a tiny child? Were you ever really even a child?
These are assumptions based on presently arising ideas.
The fact is, You simply *are* presently, and in the light of
simply *Being* it matters not whether 'already awakeness'
is recognised. As you say, presence is always the case.

Dear Nathan

I have just finished listening to your CD No One Gets
Enlightened. *I wrote the following down: 'This pure Being,
presence, awareness, aliveness is it. Everything is it! There
can't be a wrong turn—that wrong turn would be it! Doubts
are it, suffering is it. This can't be got wrong—getting it
wrong is presence being "getting it wrong".'*

*So the matter of seeing this or not seeing this, getting it
or not getting it—which seems to be the main preoccupation
of seekers (as demonstrated on the CD)—seems to be irrelevant. But yet most seekers, of course, feel that they don't see
it or get it, that there is always something to move towards.
How is this paradox resolved?*

*In other words, while awakeness may already be always
the case, the seeing of this is* not *always the case. Do you see
what I'm getting at? How is this resolved?*

Dear --------

Being or awakeness is Your true nature. Getting it or not getting it, seeing or not, makes no difference to Being, to what You *are*. Getting it or not getting it is only significant as a happening in the story of 'me'. For Being there is no resolution; none is needed.

You are this in and *as* which the play is appearing. As far as the story goes it doesn't actually matter whether the seeker 'gets it' or not. Your true nature as Being remains unaffected either way, whether or not that is known from the point of view of the character in the play.

What seems of total significance to the seeker is in reality totally insignificant. The paradox, of course, is that while the seeking is happening, that *is* reality!

Dear Nathan

There is a total resonance with what you say. I had started to attempt to answer my own question after listening to the CD again. I wrote: 'Not getting it is *presence being* not getting it!' *Is that a fair summary?*

Also, the thought came that the expression 'to get it' (see it, know it) will always suggest duality, since it implies a getter and an 'it' to get. As suggested above, not getting it is still being it (it is being the not getting it). In other words, there cannot be a seeing it—that is inherently dualistic—but there always is a being it. Does that make sense?

Finally, when you write, 'What seems of total significance to the seeker is in reality totally insignificant. The paradox, of course, is that while the seeking is happening, that is reality!', does that mean that while there is identification as a limited individual, it will always seem as though there is something to get (as you said on your CD, it's a bottomless bucket)? Whereas from the perspective of Being, so to speak, there is and never has been anything to get: it already is the case.

Dear --------

Yes, that makes sense. But with reference to your final paragraph, I would further add that the perspective of the seeker and the perspective of Being are identical, inseparable. There never actually is a seeker—the seeker is only implied by the story of seeking. But when seeking is happening, seeking *is* the reality. From that viewpoint, there is no Being—there is only seeking! In other words, Being isn't off in the background somewhere, waiting for the seeking to stop. Being *is* that seeking, totally! No other reality exists.

Dear Nathan

Something you have written has totally confused things. You say: 'From that viewpoint, there is no Being—there is only seeking!' I thought that all there is is Being, that seeking is Being being seeking. And you sort of say this later, with 'Being is *that seeking'. Surely Being is—always?*

Dear --------

Yes, you are right: seeking is Being *being* seeking. I wrote: 'From that viewpoint, there is no Being—there is only seeking!' to reinforce the point that Being isn't an entity merely hanging out in the background and being entertained in the way a member of an audience watching a play would be entertained. Rather, Being is *entirely* that play. So if seeking is the subject of the play, then Being is entirely seeking. Being and seeking in that sense are two different names for the same 'thing'.

Dear Nathan

That nails it completely. It was just a question of emphasis. It's so seductive to get carried back into the story and lose sight of things ...

I realise as I am typing that this is more of the same, but yet it's all the expression of Being. Once again it is totally and obviously clear that neither understanding nor not understanding matter. And neither does it matter whether that is clear or not!

Dear Nathan

Last Thursday I reviewed our correspondence. I read and reread it several times throughout the day. All that afternoon I felt a positive glow of well-being. The certainty of the pointers was rock solid. This was no intellectual understanding. This was a vast indestructible knowing (by no one). I sat on the floor staring out of the window in a state of completion. The certainty was rock solid and not a mind thing. If I could express it in words it would be, 'There is this one substance and everything is that. So losing the understanding or confusion are also that.'

This feeling of completion lasted three days. But now, on Monday, that recognition has a hollowness about it, like it's just a memory or an intellectual apprehension. Of course, the thought arises that this hollow recognition is oneness being hollow recognition. But somehow it doesn't feel authentic and lacks certainty. I know there is something so obvious that is staring me in the face!

Dear --------

What is staring you in the face is life as it is. Life is what it is now. *This* is oneness. *This* is Being. Maybe there's 'a vast indestructible knowing', which then switches to an understanding that appears as 'hollow recognition' with a longing for completion again.

This is the play of life, but life itself is not about *becoming* complete. Life is already complete—which may include the character's sense of feeling incomplete.

Dear Nathan

Thank you for your persistent and unwavering pointers over these past weeks.

There is the recognition that the ups and downs, the seeing it and not seeing it, the certainties and the doubts, are all part of the play. They all appear on this screen of awakeness. Yet this awakeness is never not seeing it, so to speak. This awakeness is always in the 'on' position (since 'off' would also be it).

Not seeing it is Being expressing as not seeing it. The next thought is, 'OK, but surely that needs to be seen'. This is the big error (I know that it's not an error really). Not being seen is also it!

This can't be got away from. Everything is it. Seen or not!

Phew, words just can't convey this—I don't envy you your job!

Whatever presently appears is reality

Although you talk about the life of the individual as a story,
if it seems real and in that sense is real, it has its relevance,
doesn't it? Even if it is just appearance.

Presently there's simply *this*—which may include mesmerisation with the story of 'me'. If the story of 'me' is
what appears to be real presently, then it *is* reality.

What's happening here is the describing of possibilities, and one of these possibilities is seeing that 'my life'
is a story. What's also being indicated, though, is that
seeing this is not somehow more significant than not
seeing it. The seeing of this isn't something that *has* to
happen; presently, *that* itself is another story.

Whatever presently appears is reality. It doesn't matter whether there's mesmerisation with the story of 'me'
or whether the 'me' is clearly seen to be a story. None of
it *actually* matters; it's all simply the present expression
in Being.

Why?

Why does the fictional character emerge in the first place?

Being doesn't have a reason—it simply *is*. Questions and answers can only appear because Being *is*. The question 'why?' arises as part of the appearance, and it can only be answered within the confines of a story within the appearance.

Perhaps you might ask why that tree is growing there, and I might reply with a story about a seed that fell to the ground thirty-eight years ago.

Actually, there's simply a tree there. Nothing needs to be said at all. The very appearance of the tree is something of a miracle, and in the recognition of this, any question as to the 'why' of its appearance may seem rather amusing.

The Ramana Maharshi story

Why is it that Ramana Maharshi recommends self-enquiry, while you and others like you say that nothing needs to be done?

We're concerned with actuality here, and Ramana Maharshi is just a story appearing presently in book or videotape form, albeit maybe an inspiring story. Having acknowledged that we're talking about a story, however, some interesting observations can be made about the Ramana Maharshi story.

If you trawl through a book about Ramana Maharshi, the implication of his teachings seems to be that there's karma to be overcome, knots to be undone, actions to perform, self-enquiry to undertake, etc. In amidst this assemblage of ideas and concepts and things that need to be done, here and there—as a small percentage of the total text—statements can be found along the lines of, 'The Self is already attained', or 'Right now you are the Self'.

These statements don't mean, 'Right now you are the Self but you are obliged to do self-enquiry in order to realise that'! They stand alone and mean precisely what they say. If their direct meaning is immediately obvious, then any 'hook' of instruction that may accompany them is completely ineffective in engaging attention in the story of 'me' as a separate entity. That is not, however, always the case.

Being is appearing as every character, and within this great play of life the storylines of all the various characters are played out at what appear to be different levels on a path of evolution. Therefore, whenever the assumption in a particular story is that 'I' am a distinct and separate entity that needs to straighten out my karma, do self-enquiry, meditate or whatever else seems appropriate, then that theme appears as reality.

A lack of clarity about all this gives rise to the endless bickering about how this or that way is best, and about how it is misleading to state that nothing need be done to realise what you already are, when the truth of that needs to be realised experientially. It's argued that characters who only have an intellectual understanding that nothing needs to be done may run amok doing just as they please, in the misapprehension that they are beyond retribution.

This is all, of course, based on the idea of 'me' as a separate entity, however subtle that sense of separation may be. The 'teachers' who may be making recommendations for getting rid of or transcending separation, individuality, ego, etc, are also seen as separate entities.

Whenever there's the idea that there are entities of any kind that should meditate, enquire, understand or do anything else to transcend the sense of separation, it's actually that idea of a separate entity that can do or needs to do something that reinforces—within the story—the very sense of separation it seeks to overcome.

There's also the fundamental assumption within the story that the appearance of being a separate entity is intrinsically wrong, and that any discomfort needs to be—or will be—overcome by transcending that sense of separation through enlightenment.

But everything is happening entirely of its own accord. No one is at the helm of all of this. Being appears immanently as all that is, as every character, as all of these stories of separation. All of the struggling and striving and any peace or bliss is happening in Being, as Being. This may or may not become obvious, but seeing or knowing this is not a requirement for Being. Nothing is required to *be*; confusion and separation are good enough!

So if a character reads a book on the teaching of Ramana Maharshi (or the book of any other character who appears in the play of life as a teacher, master or guru) and the idea arises that there's a need to engage in self-enquiry or meditation, or even to go to Tiruvannamalai and do *pradakshina* around Ramana's hill, then that is entirely appropriate for the unfolding of the story for that particular character. Another character may read, 'Right now you are the Self' and thenceforth live naturally in that recognition, with little or no apparent external change in their life.

All of this is happening in Being and has no significance with regard to Your nature as Being. There's only Being, so any significance is only within the story in this great play of life.

So the 'teachings' of Ramana Maharshi will be interpreted in accordance with the viewpoint from which they are perceived. They may or may not be interpreted as the especial recommendation of self-enquiry as the royal route to emancipation. Ramana's teachings contain many possibilities for an endless variety of stories.

None of it is actually leading anywhere, although it may appear that way. Your true nature is the absoluteness of Being, in appearance as all the relativity of ordinary life and spiritual seeking.

The epitome of what Ramana says does not appear as an instruction or prescription of any kind. Rather it is a *description* of Your true nature as it already is. If statements along the lines of 'Right now you are the Self' or 'The Self is already attained' resonate, then no prescription for self-enquiry or anything else will be taken seriously. If they don't resonate, then the context in which they occur *may* be taken seriously, and there will be the belief that karma needs straightening out, or self-enquiry needs to be undertaken, or whatever else seems appropriate for 'authentic' realisation.

And all of that is itself perfection. Whatever happens, there is only Being. You can't put a foot wrong, because nothing and no one is going anywhere. 'You' are not a character on a journey to self-realisation. It's all a play of appearances—including the appearance presently in word and picture form of a supposed historical character called Ramana Maharshi.

But why, if there's a real knowing that these characters are not essentially real, does the teacher speak to them as if they are real, and as if the actions they take could really have some impact on 'the path to enlightenment'? Does it show some lack of complete understanding on the part of Ramana or whoever that 'Right now you are the Self'?

Whenever there's identification as a 'me', as a separate, time-bound entity on a journey to self-realisation, then there's the assumption that Ramana Maharshi was a real person who lived in a time known as the twentieth century. It's from this perspective that the need arises to evaluate, either to defend or to criticise what Ramana said and to relate it to 'my' story. Depending (amongst other factors) on your allegiance to him, different conclusions as to whether or not his understanding was complete would then arise.

One such conclusion might be that there must have been a lack of complete understanding for him to have answered questions in the way he did, and perhaps even that he was patronising people by differentiating between those who understand and those who are in the kindergarten and still need to follow instructions.

When there's identification as 'me' and any story comes into focus as being real, as being something that *actually* happened at some time or other, then there are likely to be as many different opinions as to the 'why' of the storyline as there are characters judging it. Every opinion may seem to have some validity and—should controversy arise—is likely to be defended by its holder.

As I said at the beginning of our conversation, we're concerned with actuality here, not with justifying particular positions in relation to a story. If there isn't identification as a 'me' on 'a path to enlightenment', then it's quite obvious that the content of any story is merely entertainment; it's not something that can be considered seriously as offering a means to affect actuality in some way.

There's only presence, *what is. This* is all there is. Presence remains completely unaffected by any stories appearing in it. To *seriously* give an answer as to why

Ramana Maharshi said certain things is to reinforce the idea of time and 'other', that there is actuality beyond or outside of presence, outside of *what is*.

If there is no identification and a seeing that actually *this* is all there is, then entertaining conversations can still arise. Opinions can be traded as to why Ramana Maharshi said certain things, or why the Prince kissed the Sleeping Beauty or why the dinosaurs became extinct, without taking any of it at all seriously.

But if there is identification as 'me' and a belief that such stories are in fact reality, then it's possible that opinions will end up being defended in a blazing argument.

And, actually, that would also be perfectly fine!

There are no others

It seems clear that what's described as a person is nothing but the arising of thoughts and sensations. But why does the sense of being this particular person arise? Why these particular thoughts and sensations? Why this story?

These particular thoughts and sensations *are the only thoughts and sensations.* There *are* no 'others' with thoughts and sensations of their own that could make *these* thoughts and sensations 'particular' to 'me'. All 'others' are simply images that spontaneously arise in awareness, along with a commentary in thought that presumes or ascribes an inner someone to the images.

If the story of 'me' seems real such that thoughts and sensations do appear particular to 'me', then the story of 'you'—the story of an internal someone in another—will also seem real. If it's obvious there's no one *here,* then it will also be obvious there's no one *there.*

This seems like a kind of solipsism for no one.

It's precisely a solipsism for no one. That there are 'others' is an assumption that arises as part of the story of 'me'. All that seems to be 'me'—thoughts, sensations, etc—is presumed to similarly arise 'inside' the 'others'.

What's the actual evidence for this, though? Isn't it just an unexamined assumption, the idea that, as thoughts and sensations seem to constitute a 'someone' here, so 'others' there must have their own thoughts and sensations? What is really known of those 'others' apart from the visual images, or if a pin is stuck in one of the images, perhaps a loud noise? It's only 'known' that the 'others' have thoughts and sensations because they say they do. And what is their saying, other than an image of a mouth opening and then sounds appearing in awareness?

On the basis purely of present evidence, are there are any other thoughts and sensations anywhere at all, apart from those that arise here?

As an analogy, the characters on a movie screen relate to each other in such a way as to appear that they are actually giving thought to what they're saying. In reality, though, there are no thoughts happening inside those movie images at all. They are just visual images with a soundtrack added on. The idea that there are thoughts happening inside the images is an assumption that arises automatically when attention is absorbed in the movie in such a way that it temporarily becomes reality.

When assumptions are clearly seen as assumptions, though, they lose their potential sting.

And if the recognition arises that there are no 'others' at all, that in fact there is simply no one, this life continues to unfold in a completely natural way—*as if* there are sentient others; *as if* there is an inner life—whether rich and joyous or sad and tormented—happening inside 'them'.

What Shankara said

You say that we are already awake but that it's veiled by appearances—which to my mind equates with ignorance. So surely then we need to dispel ignorance so that we can actually know *that we are awake?*

This is a fundamental misinterpretation of what's being conveyed here. I've never said that *we* are already awake; there's no 'we' that could be awake. There are no entities—there's only Being. It's Being that's awake. Or to put it more accurately, Being is awakeness.

I have indeed said that recognition of this may be veiled by a focus on appearances as being the exclusive reality, but I haven't said that this *needs* to be overcome. Though that is certainly an idea that could be the subject matter of the story in the play.

But so long as you're assuming that you are a character in the play, there is the implication that this ignorance needs to be dispelled through self-knowledge.

When the unexamined assumption that 'I' am an actor in a play is taken to be reality, then the misconception may arise that ignorance needs to be overcome, by following a path that dispels ignorance through self-knowledge. When the 'actor' is recognised as an appearance only and it's seen that there's actually no one in the first place that any of this is happening to, what ignorance would need to be overcome?

Then it's merely an interesting—or maybe torturous—story in the play. Ignorance doesn't need to be dispelled because it's part of the storyline. Of course, the dispelling of ignorance could equally be part of the story in the play, but it would still be a play.

Being is already awake even if the story in the play doesn't include that recognition. Being isn't something that can be attained by a merely apparent someone working away at dispelling ignorance through a path of self-knowledge or whatever else.

Yes, so it's the recognition that the Self is already awake that needs to happen.

Nothing *needs* to happen.

But if truth is obscured by -

Nothing is obscured by anything. 'The truth' is not some great hidden secret that needs to be revealed through a gradual approach of acquiring knowledge. Everything is presently appearing in no-thing. That's it! That's the truth, even if that truth includes a story about ignorance that needs to be dispelled. 'The truth' is immediately and totally the case. Sounds, thoughts, sensations, visual images—whatever presently appears, along with this in which it appears—is the truth. Truth is not revealed by knowledge—it simply *is*.

But it's ignorance in the mind that hides this and that's what needs to be dispelled through jnana.

What mind is this you're talking about? It's merely another unexamined assumption that there's some thing or entity that constitutes a mind. All 'the mind' is is the flow of thought, the thought story, which in the focus on appearances as being the exclusive reality is taken to be what 'I' am.

And this will also be revealed by self-knowledge. Shankara referred to this when he said -

Scriptures aren't needed to substantiate what presently *is*. What presently is—and not what might eventually be if 'I' dispel ignorance—is what is always being pointed at here. If that's clear, then what Shankara said and the idea of paths of self-knowledge that dispel illusion will be seen as one tiny fraction of the cosmic entertainment, rather than a supreme and necessary route to emancipation.

Just the very ordinary

It seems to me that even the ease of Being you refer to in your book Already Awake *could be viewed as something out of the ordinary, and therefore something that may become the subject of seeking.*

Yes, the focus of seeking could be 'ease'.

I can only speak for myself here, of course, but I think it's important to say that seeking can *disappear, and that what's left doesn't need to be described as ease or anything else of that nature. An ordinary life is an ordinary life. Maybe that life is even extraordinary in its very ordinariness.*

How does that ordinary life manifest in your case?

Sometimes there's struggling with bodily discomfort, sometimes there's involvement with dramas and crises, and yet there's an intuitive knowing that things couldn't be any different. I literally am this body and all of its woes. In the living of life, in living it completely in all of its ordinariness, there's none of the additional tension of struggling to try to change what's happening. Things that need to get done seem to get done quite naturally. For instance, if I cut myself while I'm gardening, it seems as though it's me who has to go and get a plaster—I don't just lie on the lawn and bleed to death. Although that could happen if I was in the mood for it! (laughter)

This life has also had its share of the extraordinary, though. When I was 21, I was working in Australia where I met Swami Muktananda. I saw him several times and then received shaktipat from him. The next year I spent in total bliss. I was completely in love with Baba (Muktananda). But then I travelled back to England ... As soon as my feet touched the tarmac all hell broke loose, and the difficulties I'd experienced in my life up until I first met Baba returned with a vengeance.

I spent the next few years travelling the world, visiting and living in Baba's ashrams, meditating, chanting, serving, forever chasing that state I'd experienced in Australia.

I don't regret any of it. I love Baba to this day. I had some great adventures, I made many friends and it was very exciting being involved in that whole scene.

At the same time, though, there was always a feeling that something was missing. My body was never very strong, and in the end a life of chanting, meditating, service, working long hours—coupled with all the bliss and also all the mental anguish I often went through—it just burned me out. Eventually I settled back in England, and although I maintained my links with Baba's organisation, I was content to live a quiet life, meeting up with friends from time to time and attending satsangs with visiting teachers from around the world.

I still attend satsangs today, and occasionally I read a new book if it takes my fancy. But somewhere along the line, the interest in enlightenment completely fell away. My quiet life in this little village is all I ever really wanted. For much of the time it's characterised by a peacefulness that couldn't be equalled by the most sublime of the states of blissfulness I previously experienced. And yet I wouldn't refer to myself as *awakened, and I couldn't give a hoot whether there's an 'I' here or not.*

So even the term 'ease'—by seeming to indicate something other than life just as it is—could inadvertently promote seeking.

Yes, I take your point. However, I'm not making a prescription for ease or for the ending of seeking. What's *already* appearing is the perfect expression of Being. The talks are merely a description of this.

OK, this description/prescription thing leads me on to another point. I've read several books where the author describes their awakening to the absence of a personal self. They explain that this falling away of the sense of personal self happened spontaneously (because obviously there's no personal self that could make it happen), and then they go on to prescribe certain things that the reader can do (surrender, meditation, self-enquiry) to precipitate such a falling away! You're told that there is no personal self but nevertheless suggestions are made as to how you can get rid of your self. It all seems very misleading. Surely if it's all oneness it doesn't matter whether there's an 'I' here or not?.

Yes, it's all Being. Whatever appears is merely a play of fleeting appearances.

The idea of enlightenment seems so irrelevant now. Why be endlessly chasing what isn't? Whether there's the sense of a personal self or not, these bodies will die, and the apparent problems of a personal self aren't going to go beyond the grave.

I guess to most people it's unacceptable, living this life in an ordinary way without chasing after something better. But if the focus is on what's already happening rather than constantly looking to the future, it's obvious in a very simple way that this is actually all there is.

Unconditional apathy

What about love?

What about apathy?

I mean unconditional love.

It's all unconditional.

Memory

Does memory refer to another now?

No, there's only presence.

So it doesn't refer to another now that no longer is?

No.

What does it refer to then?

Memory is a story arising presently about what supposedly *has* happened. It has no validity apart from as a story. There is actually no history—there's only presence.

What you're saying seems just too obvious.

It *is* obvious, but when there's a belief that the story is reality it tends to get overlooked. The story diverts attention in favour of an alternative reality of past and future, where reminiscing and longing appear more attractive than unembellished direct seeing.

But outside of a talk environment I've heard you answer a question about your past.

When the story seems to be the exclusive reality, apparent suffering may arise in relation to events that appear to be happening to 'me', or in 'remembering' and anticipating such events.

But when life *isn't* viewed exclusively through the veil of thought, then living unfolds *as if* that which the story relates is real, *as if* there is a past and a future. When the story is no longer viewed as the exclusive reality, there isn't the continuity that constitutes a 'me'. So stories arise—'memory' thoughts arise—but they're not taken to be what 'I' am.

Compassion and detachment

What about compassion? If I see someone suffering I'm going to help them. As a liberated being, could you just walk away from that, just let the person die or whatever?

Everything is happening entirely spontaneously so 'help' would either be given or not, regardless of whether there was any thought story happening in relation to that.

But what's more interesting in your question is the idea that there are 'liberated beings'. Fascination with what liberation might be like is based on the initial assumption of a 'me' that can be, or needs to be, liberated—and on the further assumption that it's actually this 'me' that itself *becomes* liberated!

If that fascination should relax, it would be obvious that all ideas and speculation about liberation are based merely on unexamined assumptions.

I'll put the question differently then. Say that liberation was the case here and I didn't help someone who was suffering. There wouldn't be any agonising about that, would there?

This question is still based on the assumption of a 'me' who can be liberated. Whether or not there would be any agonising is beside the point. Once again the real issue here is the way fascination with how 'I' as a 'liberated' character might react to various situations reinforces the idea that there's someone here in the first place, and that that someone can become liberated.

I can't see the detachment in that.

What detachment?

Well, liberation is supposed to mean that there's no longer attachment to anything.

In all of this focusing on these supposed attributes of liberation, what's being overlooked is the possibility that the assumed character who feels the need to escape into liberation as an avoidance of what's presently arising isn't actually here anyway.

In presence, *this* is all there is, and the possibility of escaping present discomfort through liberation isn't entertained. Without an idealised state of liberation occupying attention, there may no longer be any impulse to change what simply *is*. Compassion and detachment and any agonising over these will be seen as part of the story of 'me'. And as it is simply a story, no liberation from it is necessary.

Everything appears because You *are*

It seems as if the difference between you and me is that there's a knowing there [pointing to Nathan] *that everything's Being, whereas there doesn't seem to be that knowing here.*

There is no 'over there'. Everything is appearing 'here' right where 'you' are—including both the image of Nathan 'there', and also the idea that there's an internal sense of being inside Nathan that 'knows'.

But Nathan sees that or knows that and I don't.

Simple presence, right 'here', is overlooked in favour of the assumption that there's an internal someone inside of Nathan 'over there'. Actually, to 'you', Nathan is a visual image and some sounds appearing in awareness. That there is life 'inside' Nathan is an assumption.

Assumptions are fine, all part of the play of life, but with such an assumption also arises a sense of lack. Life always appears to be 'out there', passing 'me' by. But actually, life is only ever happening here.

Being is always right here, the ground for the appearance of everything. Being is what You are, and without Being Nathan couldn't even appear. Everything appears because You *are*.

Identification and liberation are *both* impersonal

Nathan, whenever there's some crisis or other, the focus on it is such that identification seems inevitable. So the big story here is that life's not OK and needs to be resolved through pursuing liberation.

Liberation is not the 'answer' to problems and certainly isn't the end result of any kind of process. However, whenever there's an identification with the story of 'my' life, then quite likely that story will include the compulsion to do something about any 'problems'. Maybe then liberation is viewed as being the answer.

But how can you avoid identifying with the story?

There's no 'I' outside of the thought story that *can* avoid identifying. The 'I' that would avoid identification is an integral part of the story that arises in the play of life. And in the spontaneous seeing of this, there's no need to avoid identification: it's obvious that everything is a play of appearances arising presently in awareness.

It's not an 'I' that sees this, though. The 'I' cannot see—or avoid identifying with—anything. The 'I' is thought and thought has no capacity for action of any kind. Thoughts are just images appearing and disappearing in awareness.

So although it's not being done by any entity, identification with the images that appear in awareness may be happening. Or maybe there's clear seeing that there is no one.

And this is why liberation is impersonal, because there's no one left when it happens.

Identification is also impersonal, because there's actually no one who identifies, there's no one there in the first place! Identification happens as part of the play of life—but not to a someone. Even being a person is impersonal, because actually there are no entities at all.

But even if there's no one who identifies, identification is totally different in quality to liberation.

Whenever there's identification, there's seeming separation and an attendant sense of lack in some degree or other; a sense of something missing. What's referred to as liberation, on the other hand, is the clear seeing that there's no one—no separate entity—and therefore no such sense of lack.

But there's no one to whom either identification or liberation is happening, and no one who can bring either of them about. Identification and liberation are *both* impersonal. Both are possibilities in the play of life, and while the difference between them will appear significant, that significance is relevant only in the play.

Being is the bottom line in all of this. It is the ground that allows the expression of all possibilities and that has no dependence on any happening in the play. It is this present expression just as it appears—whether that expression should be identification or liberation. *This* is all there is.

No difference

With regard to your life story as you've previously told it to me, I must relate a similar story, that of a young man who came to a recent talk.

He said that until his mid-teen years his experience of life excluded any sense of separation. All the various characters in the play or movie of life—including himself—appeared on the screen as visually differentiated images, but there was no sense of separation in a psychological sense. Although there was a sense of location from which the movie of life was viewed, he simply didn't experience anything as other than his own being.

He lived comfortably and happily into his teen years before he realised that the 'other' characters in the movie were behaving as though bodily location was actual rather than apparent. This realisation presented something of a dilemma; it now appeared that something was wrong. It suddenly appeared as though there were a dimension of Being that was closed to him and that life would not be complete without it. Because of this perceived 'lack', his previously happy existence became a torment.

This torment continued into his early twenties, when he went to a talk on non-duality. He was amazed and relieved to discover that the lack of psychological differentiation that was natural to him was considered desirable, that the characters at the talk were actually pursuing it!

My story differs in that the recognition that 'others' experience life from the point of view of separation came to me earlier, when I was a child; my reaction to it was also different. It felt as though there were some game going on to which I was not privy, and I felt confused. All of the 'others' in the game seemed to have a purpose. They seemed to know what they were supposed to be doing, whereas I was just watching and drifting along with events.

For me, life is more like watching a movie rather than being an active participant in it. There is no sense of self in relation to others; there is consequently no standpoint for initiating actions. Everything just happens to me, or rather in me. Being for me is identical to all that is. 'I' have never had problems because there has never been a separate someone to have them, but the whole range of emotions and life circumstances—'pleasant' and 'unpleasant'—arise here just as they do wherever there's seeming identification.

Of course, as a child there was no understanding of this, just the raw living of it, and so there was a feeling of being left out, of not being in on the secret that all the 'others' shared. But just like the young man you spoke of, I too stumbled across the fact that in one way or another nearly all of the characters are seeking for liberation from the sense of separation, whereas to me the absence of separation has always been entirely natural.

Relief arose at this discovery, and now there's delight whenever I hear expressed in words what to me has always been obvious.

I can see theoretically that from the point of view of separation an event of release from that separation would probably be delightful. To me, however, the concept that there is a 'difference' between separation and oneness is a strange one, because separation is only a condition that arises as an expression of oneness, in oneness. In fact, there's never actually *any separation.*

What freedom is for me

Hi Nathan

Since a recent two-week period of self-enquiry, during which the nature of the conceptual 'I' was revealed, there has been complete freedom from suffering.

This is what freedom is for me:

The 'me' subtly softens to a character you are enjoying in the play, still navigating the world, still 'I'-ing in speech and in writing, still checking how it looks in the mirror. Having this character around is a little like having grandchildren—you are relieved of responsibility for them so you can enjoy them all the more.

Life continues as before. Before freedom you're considering permanent make-up—after freedom you're considering permanent make-up. Freedom comes most poignantly as a welcome release of suffering from compulsive self-centred thinking. The brain feels lighter, the mind is clear.

Doubts and confusion may arise for a while but they are spontaneously seen through, or they simply evaporate before seeing through becomes necessary. Old patterns which before freedom were guaranteed to push a button still arise, but the reactions are totally gone, or at least significantly reduced. Emotional pain arises, but it feels more like a sharp kind of energy; there's no story attached to it, and it quickly fades.

Joy comes and goes as a temporary experience, arising from a deep wellspring within, and a sweet peace underlies everything. The most overwhelming emotion is gratitude.

Life becomes a moment-by-moment discovery—the simplest tasks take on a new fascination—and life flows on effortlessly when there's no one there to run the show. Decisions are made as the situation requires—by no one. Action and response to arising situations occur naturally, spontaneously and compassionately. Unity is sensed more than seen. Clarity arises in reactions and responses—and always seems a little surprising.

It is a completely natural and ordinary experience, profound only in its implications. In fact, it seems so natural and ordinary that you wonder whether, if this had happened to someone who had no background in seeking, they would recognise anything 'spiritual' in it at all.

As I write this, it still seems to be triggering some experiences. Does this mean that there is still unfinished business, or is this just particular to me? My mentor is currently unavailable so I am unable to follow up with him. I'd appreciate your advice.

Dear --------

As far as the play of life is concerned, business is never finished. In this play, significance is given to the falling away of identification because of the relief experienced, but our true nature as Being is always the case under all circumstances—whether there's an 'I' or not. Being has no preference.

In the play of life, what drops away can also drop back again. If significance is given to any particular happening, then there may be disappointment if that changes. Significance given to the 'me'—or the falling away of the 'me'—indicates an entrancement with the play. But that's all right, because that's Being as well. 'Freedom' for one character will not be the same as 'freedom' for another character, but Being is all of these characters.

Within the play of life, 'freedom' may become another focus of identification. Whenever there is no particular focus on anything as having special significance, life simply is as it is. Identification or no identification, freedom or the absence of it, none of it is actually significant as far as our true nature as Being is concerned.

So what's being spoken of here is not any kind of freedom or emancipation in the life of the character—rather it's about this that already *is*, regardless of any circumstances. No need for concern then about whether there's an 'I' or not, nor for whether any process is underway, finished or not even started. Your true nature is always Being, and the play will take its own course.

Hi Nathan

I've been away for a few weeks, and things have changed a little. Now that this has settled in more, a question has come up. I have all this freedom, everything I described, and yet the experience is so ordinary that it baffles me. Where is the juice, the 'uncaused joy'? Is this everyone's experience?

All the suffering is gone, I still feel everything is arising moment by moment, I know I am present awareness. But I feel like something is missing—the God communion. There was some joy at first and now it's gone. I think people who have had some other-worldly seeing of this are better able to understand it and describe it.

I can talk about this with people. My friend now sees this, after she did the same enquiry as I did, and I helped talk her through some of the same doubts that I had. I can feel the changes in my body when I'm talking about this and that's when I feel most 'alive' with it. However, I feel like I can't authentically discuss this until I've seen through the ordinary. Does that make sense?

My mentor says not to compare my experiences with others, just to be. Does that mean there is more unfolding with this? I feel like I want to do some practices or devotional work or something to get the 'juice'.

Dear --------

Preoccupation with 'uncaused joy' and 'God communion' is just more of the story of 'me' in a different form. You say, 'I know I am present awareness but I feel like something is missing.' For as long as the 'I' continues to appear in various guises—including freedom—there will be a sense of lack. It cannot be otherwise.

'Me' as any kind of entity—even including 'me' identified as awareness—is contraction, separation, identification as some 'thing', and therefore will inevitably feel incomplete in some degree. There will always seem to be something more to acquire or attain. Maybe 'devotional work' will now happen in pursuit of 'juiciness' or 'seeing through the ordinary'.

But being 'me' isn't 'wrong'. Nothing in particular is required to *be*. 'Me' and the absence of 'me' are both happening in Being. The stories in the play of life have endless goals, including liberation, freedom and uncaused joy. Maybe some of these happen in the play (and relative to the play they will doubtless seem significant), but they are not requirements—they are just possibilities.

Maybe talking with friends in relation to the unfolding of the play happens. What's the problem with that? As a character in the play, you have as much 'authority' as any other apparent character. Don't be fooled by appearances; there are no 'liberated' characters who have an authority that 'unliberated' characters lack. So far as the play is concerned, all is appearance only.

Hi Nathan

I see why my mentor keeps telling me just to be. He said there would be this momentum of the 'me' into freedom. Time to just be, yes?

I have another question, though. My freedom came when I enquired into the arising 'me'. So when I recognise that the 'me' is returning, should I just continue my enquiry? At least for a while, so I don't get tricked again? I didn't think I could be fooled again after freedom, even though I was told to expect some continuing momentum. I guess this is why waiting is recommended before you teach.

Dear --------

It's not that the 'me' is returning—it never went away!

This importance given to the absence or presence of the 'me' is precisely what the 'me' is. What is the 'me' that would enquire? What is the 'me' that would get tricked again? Who is it that would teach?

So presently there is 'freedom'. Whatever is represented by that concept—whether it includes a 'me' or not—it doesn't need to go anywhere or turn to teaching (although it might). Being requires nothing at all—although anything might happen as an expression of Being.

Anyway, there is nothing to teach. There are simply conversations happening in Being. However directly 'Being' may seem to be a topic of such conversations, in fact *every* conversation can only actually be about Being, because Being is all there is.

So speak with your friends and advise them on the basis of your experience. Isn't that what's already happening in ordinary everyday life anyway, whatever the subject matter in question? There are no false or true teachers because there is no one—there's only Being.

On that basis, whatever happens in appearance cannot be 'wrong' because there isn't any 'right' either. There are no mistakes—there's simply *what is*.

Hi Nathan

That helps a lot—it's exactly what I needed to hear, and may need to hear again! The doer obviously isn't completely seen through, although I must say it is nice to be free of suffering. At least I know the freedom will be there always and there's no need to drop anything.

Desperation and delight

Oh no, he's back! *(laughter)*

Yes, it was quite intense last time, wasn't it? I don't have any questions left, though. Since I came to the last talk something has changed.

I remember in the introduction to Already Awake *you described an event where it seemed as though you were in a movie but without any effort being required to take part in it. That's exactly what happened here: it lasted for about three days and then gradually faded as some sense of definition returned. There was an initial feeling of disappointment, but something had changed; there was no longer the need to get an answer from 'outside'. All the questions had disappeared. As you know, I used to be a walking question mark -*

Hmm, yes. *(laughter)*

There used to be what seemed like a permanent sensation that gave rise to questions. It was like an internal itch I had to keep scratching. Since the movie event, though, as soon as any question begins to arise, it's cut off by a kind of energetic remembering of the event (as opposed to a thought-based remembering).

I don't have any intention to do this—it just happens. I can't easily define what the sense of 'me' really is any more—that's if there even is one! Certainly what previously seemed to be 'me' is gone. The intense questioning that was there before was what the 'me' was, what 'I' was. Without that there's a sense of freedom, of lightness and ease. Life isn't a burden any more. Everything is happening as before—there's still a sense of being defined by this body and by the circumstances of this person's life—but the internal nagging and questioning that was my daily torture is absent.

I came here today for the sheer delight in hearing you talking about all of this, rather than in a desperate attempt to get something out of it.

Well, you certainly seem a lot more relaxed than usual.

Yes, I think I'm a lot easier to be around now! (laughter and cheers)

Cause and effect

Isn't there a danger that as a result of hearing that there is no cause and effect, someone could start behaving in ways that are anti-social and inhumane and even cause harm to other people?

You mean, someone goes to a talk on non-duality and as a result he suddenly becomes a daredevil ruthless criminal? *(laughter)* You're saying that without the idea of cause and effect as a protecting factor you might go and rob a bank? Because there's no one there so it wouldn't matter?

Well yes, exactly.

And so if there's no one there, it wouldn't matter if 'no one' went to prison either, would it?

Well, um ... no. (laughter)

The *idea* that there's no cause and effect is different to clearly seeing that there's no one to whom cause and effect pertain.

When there's mesmerisation, such that the story of 'me' as an individual appears as reality, cause and effect is implicit in that story. And it's certainly possible that the story of 'me' as an individual could unfold in such a way that there does appear to be irresponsible behaviour, seemingly as a result of hearing that there's no cause and effect.

But if the story is seen *as* a story, then the 'me' that forms part of that story quite clearly arises spontaneously, and whatever happens in the story isn't being 'done' by anyone.

Shouldn't it be the case that if I come to a talk like this and hear that I'm no one and everyone, then that would completely remove any tendency to want to harm another in any way? After all, if I did, I'd only be harming myself.

If it appears as a communication to 'me' as a character, then it might make no difference at all. If it's clearly seen that there's no one—no 'me' and no 'others', that all is simply a play of appearances—in that case the question wouldn't even arise.

But going back to your original question: as it happens I've never heard of *anyone* rushing out of a talk or satsang to commit an atrocity. If you do, it'll be a first. *(laughter)*

Right! All I need is a gun. (laughter)

Difference is relative

There have been instances of a falling away of the 'me' here, and it feels very different when life is viewed from that perspective rather than from the point of view of identification.

Yes, of course, but 'differences' only relate to the play of life, to appearances and content. Being, the context, remains unchanged, regardless of appearances.

But if such a shift in perception happens (even if only temporarily), perspective may be totally transformed.

Yes.

And from the point of view of the identified 'me', that shift in perception is what is pursued as enlightenment.

Yes.

So from the point of view of the 'me' again, this shift is something that has to happen.

From the point of view of the 'me', yes, it is usually seen as important and desirable that such a shift should happen. (It's by no means a certainty, though, that such a shift *will* happen; it's simply another possibility in the play of life.) But it's *only* from the viewpoint of identification that such a shift appears as something important, as something that *must* happen. Whether there's identification or not, whether there's a shift of any kind or not, Your true nature is always Being.

But if a shift in perception happens and there's no longer identification as a 'me' but rather a seeing that there's actually no one here, that's bound to seem significant.

But it will also be seen that actually, identification or not, there's *only* Being, in and as which all of this is happening. Importance and significance go hand in hand with identification.

Right, yes. So from the perspective of identification, it's always going to seem as though something significant needs to happen. And something might happen ... But that happening—however significant it might seem—doesn't touch Being.

Precisely. In the absence of identification, nothing is significant because there's nothing 'else' for anything to be significant in relation to.

I see what you're saying: nothing can make any difference to the absoluteness of Being. But of course while there is identification, then everything's still relative, and the falling away of identification is always going to seem to be something that needs to be attained before there can be peace. That's what seeking for enlightenment is.

That's right. There can, however, be a clear understanding of what's being said here, and although understanding doesn't remove the sense of identity, it can put seeking into perspective, such that the desperation or anguish that often arises in relation to blind seeking vanishes.

So what is that sense of identity dependent on? What can remove it?

Well, from the perspective of identification, it seems, of course, as though there's a 'me' here that can do things, that is capable of causing effects. In the absence of identification, though, it's obvious that there's no one doing anything. Everything is happening entirely of its own accord—including identification and the absence of identification. Identification isn't caused, and its disappearance isn't the effect of any cause.

So the falling away of identification quite simply either happens or doesn't happen. There can't be any control over it because, even if appearances indicate otherwise, there's no one here making anything happen anyway.

Precisely so.

Advaita

What is 'neo' advaita in relation to traditional advaita?

I don't know, I've never heard of it. Pass that one to the scholars; best leave the scripture and history to them. *What is* is only present. You'll need a story about time in order to translate scriptures and practices into future enlightenment.

(2nd speaker) *Nathan, can I relay a quote attributed to Shankara?*

Go ahead.

'Study of the scriptures is fruitless as long as Brahman has not been experienced. And when Brahman has been experienced, it is useless to read scriptures.'

Actually, as there's *only* the experiencing of Brahman it's probably fine to read the scriptures if you've run out of novels. *(laughter)*

I've got another quote; one from Ramana Maharshi.

Who needs a book when you're about? *(laughter)* Let's have it then.

'There is no greater mystery than this: ourselves being the Reality, we seek to gain Reality. We think there is something

hiding our Reality and that it must be destroyed before the Reality is gained. That is ridiculous. A day will dawn when you will yourself laugh at your past efforts. That which will be the day you laugh is also here and now.'

Amen to that! (laughter)

Choice and consequence

Don't these characters seemingly make choices that appear to have consequences?

It certainly can appear that way.

So there are choices and consequences, aren't there?

That's merely one way of viewing reality. It's only when there's exclusive viewing through the filter of thought that there seems to be a psychologically-based subjective entity that's making choices.

But I believe that the reason I'm sitting here now is a consequence of previous thoughts and choices getting me here. I've heard you say that whatever presently appears is reality. So if that seems real to me it must be real.

What presently appears *is* real: the visual image of this room full of people, sensations arising in the body, the sound of aircraft ... and also any thoughts that may be arising. But when reality is viewed through the filter of thought, it appears differently from when thought is seen as just another aspect of the whole picture.

Thoughts are like speech bubbles in a comic. When you merely *look* at a comic, you see the pictures and you see the speech bubbles. When you *read* the comic, you enter into the world that the words in the speech bubbles appear to create, and that can become more meaningful, more the reality if you like, than the pictures. And that's analogous with what is referred to as the psychological dimension, where this sense of separation appears.

What I don't understand is why the thought story is said to be less real than, say, sensations or visual images. I don't see why there should be this distinction. Why should how we seem to live our lives, cause and effect and all the rest of it, be an illusion and just presentness be real?

When the thought story is taken as exclusive reality, its effect is to divide and fragment. 'I' appear as a distinct entity subject to time—which further implies cause and effect. In that sense, what presently appears *is* real but it's being viewed in a fragmented way.

I understand what you mean: that your thoughts can completely cloud over what is happening or give a different slant to it. But I still don't see why there should be this hierarchy, if you like, where the simple sensory data that arise in presence seem to be somehow superior to the thought story.

There isn't a hierarchy.

In that case, if thought in any form is no better or worse than anything else, why are you saying there's no cause and effect?

Thoughts are appearing in presence—presence isn't appearing in thoughts. When reality is viewed through the filter of thought then there's the *idea* of causation;

the idea that this present configuration of appearances has been caused by past effects. Actually, though, if it wasn't for simple presence, there couldn't *be* any thought.

In the thought-filtered view there are endless possibilities. There can be anything you like, anything at all: cause and effect, choice and consequence, different realms, future, past, you name it. But as this view is limited to thought alone—which is merely a fraction of the totality of present appearances—the view is inevitably partial. It's merely part of the *whole* picture, and confinement to it produces a sense of lack, with an attendant seeking for wholeness.

However, if a fragmentary world *does* appear as reality, then indeed it *is* so, and in that case it's wholeness that appears illusory! It's not that the causal view is wrong, but it's only one way of perceiving things.

When thoughts are seen as thoughts and the viewpoint derived from them isn't assumed to be exclusive, there's simply presence, with no time and therefore no cause and effect.

Self-enquiry

Can self-enquiry lead to liberation?

There's no one bound and therefore no liberation from bondage. What you're referring to as liberation is the seeing or knowing of this. But a story about bondage may spontaneously appear in Being, and that story could include a theme of liberation through self-enquiry.

So in the story of self-enquiry, can liberation happen?

The story of liberation through self-enquiry unfolds in such a way that there is the *impression* of an entity becoming less bound as the story weakens, seemingly as a 'result' of self-enquiry. But the entity that apparently dissolves isn't really there in the first place; it's merely suggested by the story. Maybe at some point in the story this becomes transparently obvious, but until that point enquiry appears as a serious endeavour on the part of an apparent entity.

When it is transparently obvious that there are no entities that are bound, then efforts toward liberation through enquiry or any other means become a joke.

Why then do supposedly liberated beings recommend enquiry?

There are neither liberated beings nor beings that are

bound; there's only Being. But so long as the story seems real, there may well appear to be 'other' beings who offer instruction.

If the story is transparent and it's obvious that there's no one bound—and therefore no one needing liberation—what serious consideration could be given to the 'liberated' status of a merely *apparent* 'other' or to any admonition from that 'other' to undertake self-enquiry?

It's a red herring then.

If there's a story that includes the urge toward liberation through enquiry, then the story may well continue to unfold in that way, regardless of whether I declare it to be a red herring or not. However, if the story includes being told that enquiry is a red herring and the story becomes transparent as a seeming result of that, then enquiry is indeed seen as a red herring.

There's also another answer to your question as to why supposedly liberated beings recommend enquiry. If 'I' as a character in the story experience what 'I' believe to be liberation as a 'result' of enquiry, 'I' may then proceed to teach enquiry as a means of liberation to that which is still perceived as 'others'.

How would you know if you were really liberated or not then?

If 'I' am teaching 'others', then the story is well underway. But as it's most likely a fairly comfortable story by then, 'I' probably wouldn't care anyway!

But what about the others who are being taught by someone who isn't really liberated?

There aren't any others! The delusion here lies in the idea that 'I' am a teacher.

Personal liberation

I think my old aunt must be liberated. She's had all sorts of difficulties in her life but she says now that after a while you just don't care any more. (laughter)

Many of the characters who come to the talks are in this kind of position. There can often be a story where, through experience of life, the sense of personal self no longer appears in relation to much of what arises.

Everything comes up to be seen for what it is.

Yes. Maybe there's no reaction to certain happenings in life, so no sense of personal self arises in response.

But where there *is* a reaction, what appears as the response is in fact the 'me'. So it could be said that the response is in a sense what the 'me' actually is. This is then played out as life simply living itself as a 'me' in relation to situations, until maybe the sense of personal self no longer arises.

That all sounds a bit bland, though. I want liberation to be something more than life just living itself out.

Maybe you want 'personal' liberation.

Actually, I don't even know if it's liberation that I'm looking for.

Perhaps you just want to be always having a good time.

Well, yes. (laughter)

That's often what the idea of liberation is. There's a subtle idea of a 'me' that will be liberated into having an endlessly good time, rather than there being a total absence of a 'me' that needs to be, or could be, liberated.

So going back to the way the sense of a personal self appears as a response to what arises. Let's say a 'me' is appearing in relation to financial issues which gets translated into the desire for liberation as an escape from the situation, and then you come to the talks in pursuit of this. If you win the lottery tonight, would you bother coming back to another talk?

No I wouldn't. And anyway, how did you know why I'm here? (laughter)

Wow!

But Nathan, even when there's a story and emotions, they are there—they're real.

Exactly. That *is* reality. If there's total confusion, then precisely *that* is reality.

And that's fine, isn't it? Part of me seems to be hoping that I'll hear something that gets rid of the sense of identification, but the rest of me is quite happily sitting here hearing that the identification is perfectly OK. While there is a concept that somehow the story and all that stuff should be falling away, that there should just be this sense of Beingness, the beauty of what you're saying is that all of that is Being already.

Yes, completely.

If there's struggling going on, then that's it as well.

Any struggling is it as well. There's nothing that isn't reality. There's only Being.

Wow! I just feel like ... God ... (laughter) Thank you. Oh! I didn't mean I feel like God. (laughter)

Well, as it happens ... *(laughter)*

Other titles from Non-Duality Press include:

Nathan Gill
Already Awake

Leo Hartong:
Awakening to the Dream
From Self to Self

John Wheeler
Shining in Plain View
Awakening to the Natural State
Right Here, Right Now

'Sailor' Bob Adamson
What's Wrong with Right Now?
Presence-Awareness

John Greven
Oneness

Richard Sylvester
I Hope You Die Soon

Printed in the United States
117734LV00002B/343/A

9 780955 176227